Praise f... D1504302

Kim's latest book *Soul Power* will magically destroy your ignorant state of mind and gift you with a pure intellect strengthened by faith and filled with overflowing love... Her book is easy to absorb and extremely valuable in this day and time... Check it out and you will be surprised...

—**Sri Vishwanath**, author of *The Secret of Bhagavad Gita*, and *The Magic of God*, founder of *Bhagavad Gita University*

Visually beautiful. At first, the simplicity of the wisdom inspired me the way many wise teachings do, opening my mind and reminding me what is already inside me. But then, I noticed that the words were seeping into my soul in another way—not just inspiring but actually being part of a change in my breathing and in the way I perceived my life. I felt like I was walking into a more beautiful life.

—**Rosanne Finn**, author of *The Whirling Dance of Planets*, and *Journey-work of the Stars*

This is a book to keep near you and visit often. It is clear, concise, and full of inspired truth. *Soul Power* is a friend that will help in keeping you on the path of loving kindness, and one which has the capacity to guide you back when you have become dull, anxious, or exhausted, having forgotten the truth of who you are. Her words are profound truth, in a language that all can understand: I am the radical love of my soul's desire!

—**Murshida Leilah Be**, *Sufi Ruhaniat Order International*

This book is a powerful and exquisitely crafted prescription for living authentically, in alignment with, and fully expressing, our inherent spiritual qualities and essential nature. Kim has integrated the wisdom of many healing and spiritual traditions to offer a clear and precise path for integrating spirit and matter, through the psyche, viscera, and soul. Each chapter deepens our understanding of a specific quality of love and offers "love notes," which inspire sacred connection and point to profound yet practical truths. *Soul Power* provides the tools, insights, and loving support to directly realize our precious, innermost essence. This book is truly a much-needed gift to the world.

—**Carol Alena Aronoff, Ph.D.** author of *Compassionate Healing: Eastern Perspectives; Cornsilk; The Nature of Music; Her Soup Made the Moon Weep; Blessings from an Unseen World; Dreaming Earth's Body; Tapestry of Secrets*

Soul Power's abundant quotes on courage, gratitude, truth, wisdom, and compassion invite each of us to "Be the Love" the Divine has gifted us to be, to be our core self.

—Gratefully, **Sister Lucy Wynkoop**, Order of Saint Benedict, Saint Placid's Priory, *The Priory Spirituality Center*

Soul Power is a step-by-step instruction guide of how to live a passionate and powerful life. It is written with great clarity and sequence to allow the audience to integrate the information. It is a practical guide to living a soulful life!

—**Anna Boatright**, founder of *Beloved Sanctuary* and creator of *Be*

This is a guide that we can use to help ease the ego's resistance to a new level of felt knowledge, and I'm so grateful that she is creating this body of knowledge.

—**Heather Flournoy**, founder of *Hudson Valley Healing and Meditation with Horses*

This work has helped me! It has helped me see me. It has helped me engage me in new ways, see myself differently, and relate to people in fresh ways. Long story short, this work has given me a reason to live! I felt that I didn't belong here because of childhood, race, and Vietnam War trauma. When I first started working with Kim Lincoln, I stumbled through explaining my trauma. Through our work I have learned I do not need to explain it, but I need to have the courage to be with it and presence it through my body. I've learned from Kim that the body wants to be heard, listened to, felt, and engaged. There is a power in the vulnerability of our body's music and song.

—**Dr. David Whitfield**, *Intercultural Leadership Executive Coaching; Adjunct Professor, Doctoral Program in Leadership Studies at Gonzaga U.*

Imagine you are taking a stroll in a garden in the evening. The sun is shedding its final rays and exotic blooms share their fragrance with you. *Soul Power* is a walk in such a garden of mystical delights. In *Soul Power*, Kim Lincoln brings a spirit of inquiry that illuminates our deepest, most subtle essences. This is a delightful and rewarding exercise that will guide you in your own personal journey of the soul.

—**David Hanig MSW**, *Poet*

Kim speaks of soul power with a simple eloquence born of lived experience. She knows the living truth of the soul's power and guides the reader to know this power intimately and directly through the deep clarity of her soul's call.

—**Dr. Heather Taylor-Zimmerman PhD,** founder of *The Soul of Creativity*

SOUL POWER
You Loving You

by Kim Lincoln

 A gift for you

Dear Mia, Here is a book I got for you.
Love, Alan

WHITE LION Olympia, Washington

Soul Power, You Loving You

Author: Kim Lincoln

Editor: Marye Hefty

Cover Design, graphics and layout: C. Buck Reynolds

Copyright © 2020 by Kim Lincoln

Interior Photo: Anna Boatright

Back Cover Head Shot Photo: Silver Wolf

KDP Independent Publishing Platform, North Charleston, SC

First published in 2020 by
White Lion Publishing, LLC
6227 Northill Dr. SW
Olympia, WA 98512

ISBN – 978-1-7348065-0-2

Self-Transformation/ Spirituality/Self-Help

The views offered here are the sole opinions of the author. They are in no way a substitute for sound medical advice, nor are they intended to prescribe. All matters regarding your health require medical or psychological supervision. Neither the author nor the publisher shall be liable or responsible for any loss or damage allegedly arising from any information or suggestion made in this book. The author is held harmless against any unintended encroachment upon another author's opinion. Any part that is known to belong to another has been documented here. Certain words such as "presencing" are those of the author's own work and her teacher's work and not necessarily comparable to current usage in American English. The English language offers very few words to describe the nature of this work, and so terms used here may sound like, but not necessarily mean the same thing as, the use of such words in other contexts.

Table of Contents

Gratitude & Dedication

To the One Perfection
Divine Source

My eternal appreciation to Faisal Muqaddam
for his masterful inquiry into essence and for
sharing with me the greatest gift of my life.

Dedicated to my dad Bob Lincoln and his
lovely wife Sharon. I imagined you sitting with
me as I wrote. This book is for you!

And to my editor, Marye Hefty,
and to my designer Carolyn Reynolds,
a tremendous heartfelt "thank you."

Foreword

Forewords are usually written by experts within the field who share their support for a book. Kim Lincoln could have asked an expert in somatic and energy healing to write the foreword to this book. However, she asked me, one of her students, to introduce this work. I am not surprised because a major premise of her work is to learn to quiet our ego and be with our essence, our soul power, which is not big, or puffed up, or important, but still and vast and containing.

What I appreciate about Kim's teachings and classes is that she is not saying "follow me." She is also not teaching to leave one's faith tradition (whether this be Jewish, Christian, Buddhist, Native American, Wicca, etc.). Instead, she is teaching that each of our individual spiritual paths (whether we are aware we are spiritual beings or not) can be enhanced if we learn how to be fully human.

This "being fully human," which I practice in her classes, involves learning to be present with (aware of) the sensations in my body and not just living from my mind. For example, before taking Kim's classes, when I experienced a feeling that I labeled a negative emotion, like sadness, I might have read positive quotes or told myself not to wallow in this feeling. Now, I have learned that at appropriate times (maybe in meditation after work or during a lunchtime walk) to let the feeling be felt in my body and to be curious about what the resulting sensations feel like. In practicing this, I am experiencing feelings that used to frighten me, now passing through me like weather. which is a simile she often uses in her classes. I am experiencing more kindness toward myself. I no longer judge myself harshly when I feel sad or mad or frustrated. Instead, I am learning to be curious and to listen to my body. As a result, I am finding I have more patience and understanding for my friends, family, and even strangers. I am learning that my energy is valuable and powerful and connected to a larger consciousness. I am learning to accept and include my body, and not just my mind, in my spiritual journey.

Soul Power is Kim's gift to her students and to any spiritual seeker. The love notes in this book are nuggets from her classes and over 40 years of intensive studying and teaching. There is a profound depth in their simplicity. Her message is simple and complex at the same time: The power of the soul is in being fully human, and being fully human means experiencing all of our humanness. Our spiritual path is our human path.

Thank you Kim, from one of many students (who is speaking for many of your students).

Editorial Notes

Soul power is accessed by being present in our own unique essence, and in so doing, we simultaneously tap into an essence that is bigger than us and connects us all. Faith traditions have different terms for this universal essence that is both accessible in us, through us, and outside of us from a source that is greater than us. It is as challenging to explain as quantum physics, but seekers of all faith traditions understand it. Some of the terms used by these faith traditions include God, the Light, Allah, Christ, Buddha Nature, Mother Earth, the Divine, the Universe, Source, the Supreme Being, Creation, the Still Small Voice, and other terms that have this sense of a spiritual presence within us and connecting us. For grammatical consistency, my editor asked me to select one term for this concept; however, at the risk of being grammatically inconsistent, I am applying these terms interchangeably in ways that honor all seekers on their paths and all of our connections. Also, when I write a grammatically singular noun (such as "soul") with the plural possessive pronoun "our," this refers to an individual aligned with the collective source, so in this book, it is not "my soul" but "our soul."

Introduction

Through presencing the sensations in our bodies in relation to our interactions within the world, we can access the subtlest, most delicate yet strengthening love—the Lataif. Originating from a Persian word before the time of Rumi, Lataif means the subtle breath (body) of the soul. This language of our soul is the felt sense of this subtle body and a simultaneous open awareness that are both accessed through our refined perceptual knowing. In this way and with practice, we can evolve, becoming conscious of and claiming what is beyond our conditioning. — Kim Lincoln

The Soul is Our Inner Guide

I have spent over 40 years studying the soul's interplay with the body, mind, and emotions. This book *Soul Power* contains my high-vibrational love notes distilled from these years of study, my private practice, and teaching. It is a book designed to support soul growth and our daily practice of staying open to life without judgement and with courageous curiosity.

This work involves being with our own essence.[1] This means welcoming all feelings into our body and presencing these feelings in ways that allow them to process through (and not get stuck) in the body—like witnessing the changing weather —and just being with what is, seeing what is, and letting

---

[1] Essence in my teaching means love. It is that place where the Divine Light in our soul meets our body.

it pass through without judgement. Within such presencing, we grow compassion for ourselves as we truly experience who we are in each moment as both limitless and limited, loving and selfish, and the full range of other human experience.

And, once we learn empathy for ourselves, soul growth requires an empathy for one another and all creatures. This requires our soul power. It is to be empowered by what is bigger than just me and you. Each one of us is called to grow up and show up in ways that we have not known before and to be willing to grow and change and include each other. To do this invites us to begin to know and to surrender to the loving nature of our being and to the loving Grace inherent in the world and universe within and around us.

Please use this book in whatever way feeds your soul:

- Read it slowly from cover to cover as a soothing balm of higher vibrational frequency.

- Read a chapter when you need support in accessing a specific virtue.

- Read randomly by opening a page each day and using these words during your meditation as a reminder to be more present.

- Read or copy one of the notes for a family member or friend to tell them how they embody this virtue.

Background and Book Organization

The title of each chapter is a virtue of the soul—courage, gratitude, truth, wisdom, and compassion, and each virtue is a quality of love. These virtues are directly connected to and affected through the choices we make. For example, while stuck in traffic, I can choose to breathe calmly and to feel the frustration of being stuck. I can choose not to project my frustration onto another driver but instead to breathe through my frustrated feelings and presence them. In this way, I can get in touch with my possible impatience, and this may provide me with some insights. Also, there is the possibility by being present with this, that I can process through this feeling of frustration, and as a result feel more open, receptive, and less stressed. Whereas, if I choose to project anger at the cars in front of me, my body may constrict, and I may react in ways that do not help the situation. In every moment, I have a choice.

In our goal-oriented culture, it can be challenging to "do" soul work. I have found one thing that helps me to embrace my humanness in all of this — to realize it is more like practicing a sport or a musical instrument. As a former ballet dancer, I like to think of soul work as the daily practice I did to perform. I never "arrived" and then could rest on this talent. I had to practice daily, and I loved it, although it was hard.

Another aspect that helps me embrace my humanness in the process is to think of soul work as having seasons. Nature's cycles—rest, renewal, budding, fruiting, expiration—directly mirror the very same progression needed to support personal growth. This cycle supports the flowering of our consciousness while simultaneously providing the holding environment necessary to feel safe in letting go of what is no longer needed in order to develop and grow. In soul work, what can feel like dying is in fact an essential preparation necessary to provide the nutrients needed to enrich our growth.

Just like nature, the soul too is of nature. The nature of the soul is the witnessing part of us that stays with us through all of our life no matter what. The soul will not abandon us. It is a true friend who is a pure part of us without agenda. It comes from Divine Light, yet it is denser than light and is subtler than the body. The soul is essential for the mind and body to grow. It is the neutral witness of the material that is our thoughts, emotions, and instincts. The soul refines our experiences and takes the essences of our experiences back into the Light.

My hope is that this book is a reminder, especially during challenging times, that we are all (each of us) the love we need, and that the world needs our love and soul growth.

Let us all light up our own soul power, and together light up this world.

Like a lamp of oil that burns—
The flame is the Light of Spirit (chakra).
The wick is the essence of love (lataif).
The lamp is the oil of the soul (essential nature).

How does this relate to our daily life?
Simple.

Our mind when open is the Light.
Our heart when open is the wick.
Our body when open is the container that generates the fuel.

Each aspect is interconnected with another.
And each of us is connected to one and another.

— Kim Lincoln

As with fine tea, steep in these words,
and slow your pace until your thirst is quenched.
Savor this subtle realm in welcoming a gentler time and place.
Linger with each love note as though spoken by you to yourself.

Courage

$\mathcal{S}$oul Power is
you loving you.

$\mathcal{B}e$ $\mathcal{L}oved.$

It is letting go
and embracing the love
that is your essence.

Beloved.

Soul Power is
drawing upon
this inner strength to live
your life courageously.

Be Courageous.

$\mathcal{I}$t is knowing that

what you want wants you.

It is knowing that

the love you want is already inside you.

$\mathcal{K}$now $\mathcal{T}$his.

Nobody can give you
what you already have.
The love you feel for another
is your love.

Be the Love . . .

*for you are a love song
of God's creation.*

You are a one-of-a-kind
Divine expression
all your own.

You Matter.

Soul Power is
living in your own skin
and being fully present here.

Be Here.

It is loving your life
and living the passion
of your unique expression.

Be Uniquely You.

$\mathcal{S}$oul Power is
having the capacity
to embrace all of you.

Embrace It All.

It is stretching in ways

you have not stretched before

to grow courageously

where you dared not go.

Be Daring . . .

for you have opened your heart

to include all of life. Be jeweled

in all its fullness.

Soul Power is
being embodied and
letting be felt what
has lain hidden.

Be Embodied.

$\mathcal{W}$elcome misunderstandings.

Welcome shortcomings.

Welcome the innocence

that doesn't know another way.

Be Welcomed.

Soul Power is
being free of
letting anyone else's feelings
define who you are.

Free Yourself.

$\mathcal{I}$t is releasing any shame
about having strong emotions
and pleasurable sensations.

Release Shame.

Soul Power is
allowing the raw energy
to cycle through you
like a wildfire
spreading in your body.

Feel the Warmth . . .

*for only you can do this part
to be a loving partner to yourself.
Fall in love.*

Soul Power is
embracing your
life-force energy
to feel fully alive.

Be Enlivened.

It is the capacity to land

in your skin and

not jump outside of yourself

when you feel uncomfortable.

Grow Your Capacity.

Soul Power is
having the maturity
not to make your discomfort
about somebody or something else.

Grow Up.

It is understanding

that what you react to in another

resides in you.

Own what is yours.

Own It.

*I*t is knowing

that reactivity is a charge.

Be with the charge.

Be responsible for what you feel.

Feel It . . .

for you are creating new habitat.
Burn in your wildfire until the
elements transmute. Allow what
drives the fire to be seen and felt.
Purify your emotions.

C harge exists
where charge persists
and what persists
you get more of.

Know Like Attracts Like.

*S*oul Power is
knowing that resonance
attracts the same resonance.
What you vibrate is amplified.

Be Aware.

It is realizing that reactivity
reinforces re-action.
The more you react
the more reaction you get.

Release Reactivity.

Soul Power is
having the strength
to raise anger to passion
and to move that energy
into positive action.

Be Proactive.

It is learning to
stand on your own two feet
and rise
when you have fallen.

Step Up ...

*for you are the dream that
dreamt you alive inspired by
the life you desire.*

$\mathcal{S}$oul Power is
intoxicating love.
It is the pure expression
of spirit's passion.

Feel the Passion.

It is passionately
cherishing any part of you
that you want another to feel
about you.

Cherish Yourself.

Soul Power is
courageously connecting with
and engaging with
what only you can create.

Be Creative.

$\mathcal{I}$t is fully expressing yourself
and having your extraordinary life
in ordinary ways.

Express Your Life.

Soul Power is your power.
It is living the love
of your authentic self.

Live the Love . . .

*for you are the radical love of your
Soul's desire. Be authentically you.*

Courage is the passion to live our life authentically. It is the spirit of embodying our unique, one-of-a-kind beauty and expressing ourselves fully. It takes courage to embrace one's self and cherish one's self. It takes courage to have the strength to be our own person in our own skin, and consciously feel the vibrancy of our soul, which is created through the aliveness of our fire bejeweled with our life-force energy.

Courage is the self-loving determination and freedom we grant ourselves to individuate from emotionally driven habits. Instead, we partner with our higher vibration by skillfully tolerating the visceral charge of sensations in a mindful manner. Here, the true essence of our spirit is revealed, transforming matter into the pure expression of our soul.

So, how do we access courage and find the strength to individuate and become true to our authentic self?

Through self-love. Self-love provides the strength to be with any emotional and physical momentum that drives addictive behavior. Addiction is the craving compulsion of dependency on a substance, activity, person, or thing that we ingest or merge with habitually. This kind of attachment is so enmeshed that it can be difficult to separate from it without feeling failure, betrayal, anger, or shame. This is because in so doing, it exposes what our addiction or external attraction covered up and what we were afraid to feel.

Addictive or grasping behavior tethers us to something or someone to satisfy our want in order to give us an artificial feeling of being held. Being held is what we needed as an infant. Our earliest memories of being held are impressed in our body's memory. For example, when we teethed or cried, we wanted to be held and soothed. As an infant, we learned how to regulate our emotions and the building charge in our body through the felt experience of our care provider (often a mother) holding, rocking, and comforting us. This enabled us to learn how to melt through the charge and feel pleasurable connection. In this way, we learned how to feel connected both with another and within ourselves.

Yet, if our caregiver was distracted, disinterested, or inappropriate, and we were left to emote without our needs being met, we likely may have developed anxiety about touch, over-reactivity, depression, or issues with food, or substances, etc., driven by frustration, anger, and ultimately the hurt of feeling unwanted. As we grew up, we may have sought pleasure through other means in order to feel that yummy merged and connected feeling.

So, now, as an adult, any attempt to separate from an addictive behavior, or excessive attachment, whether it be to food, emotionality, alcohol, drugs (legal or illegal), sex, poor relationships, etc., is met with an uncomfortable visceral charge that is prickly, agitating, annoying, or consuming. This visceral charge is because we have not learned how to circulate the dynamic and intense charge within the self that accompanies our basic needs and that wants to be met in order to soothe this agitation for us.

Unfortunately, if we try to satisfy this charge or diminish its intensity by making it about needing another to give us what we want (or needing to be needed, or betraying one's self by not allowing one's self to have what we want) our attempts for satisfaction and satiation will fail to be fulfilled. Our dissatisfaction will grow with anger, aggression, hostility, and even revenge, hurting ourselves or hurting others because they will never give us enough. The answer is not outside of us.

The truth is that no person, or anything external, can sustain our desire to be satisfied by filling in for us what is ours to claim in our self. Addictive, grasping, and avoidant behaviors are distortions concerning connection. We are actually craving that first connection that our mothers were meant to mirror for us, which teaches us how to be genuinely loving and embodied human beings, comfortable in our own skin. Yet, even the most perfect mother cannot ultimately give us our connection to Source.

Now, it is up to us to connect in a loving way with our self. So, courage is what is needed. This is the courage to feel the emotions that we are feeling and to be able to inhabit uncomfortable sensations in the body without acting them out inappropriately or blaming another for how we feel. With courage, now it is time for us to mother our self by both feeling the charge and cultivating for our self our own self-loving holding. Yet, this is not to say that we do not need others; rather, it is to say that we do not use others to do what is waiting for us to develop and be for our own self.

So, how do we do this? In this example, if we feel irritated or scratchy, we may be feeling frustrated about getting whatever it is that we want in the way that we want it. First, we need to acknowledge the issue, and then be with and own the feeling of that charge. When we can identify the issue and feel it, we next need to muster the courage to not only feel it but also to not become identified with it as who we are. For example, we may feel the emotion of sadness. Like a wave, this emotion will rise and fall. We are not sadness. This whole perspective requires mindfulness and objectivity. It means to not identify with the charge as who we are but to cultivate the ability to understand that the charge is a reaction and that reaction is not the core self, meaning the true self. If we do not see this distinction, we may fall into shame and defensiveness. When we act out defensively, we are actually intensifying the uncomfortable sensation by adding fuel to the flame and escalating it even more.

The skill is to learn to tolerate the charge. It is to have the courage to feel the charge without acting it out in an inappropriate way that hurts our self or others. So then, how do we feel it and yet have enough distance? If we get closer into the charge, we will escalate it. What is needed is to feel it and at the same time witness it with curiosity and a broader perspective. This witnessing awareness of the charge is literally feeling it while simultaneously being aware of the space and energies outside of us. This enables us to learn with practice how to be with and to regulate the charge. Learning to tolerate emotional and visceral charge is at the root of transmuting entangled energies into charismatic energy that can serve us in so many ways.

Once we are adept at this, then we can move in closer to the fire, which is our spiritual connection. Here we are learning to separate what is real from learned behavior. We learn to recognize our essence. We learn to live our life passionately and whole-heartedly. This requires of us the courage to individuate and be our own person. Stepping out into the world from here cultivates a sense of "I can."

Our soul purpose is having the courage to rise-up with self-loving expression from our heart's desire.

Courage is the strength to sit in the heart of our soul's fire. It requires we let burn away and purify any desire that is not of the true self. This is the paradox. The test is—if the passion is of the ego, emotionality will intensify. If the passion is of our true self, it will become an ember of burning desire that fuels authentic action. For when passion is from the true self, it is an eternally burning ember. Here you are the love, loved, and your beloved. This is the request of courage: allow yourself to be loved.

Gratitude

Soul Power is
an infinite fountain
of goodness and grace.

Be Graced.

It is

a well-spring of love

spontaneously arising

from your grateful heart.

Love Gratefully.

Soul Power is

fully receiving

the gift of life

no matter how it appears—

empty or full.

Receive the Gift.

It is appreciating

the great fullness

of the glass itself

being held by what is more.

Be the Container.

Soul Power is new life,
celebrating, integrating, unifying
mind-body-heart and soul
—every cell of your being.

Be Happy . . .

for yours is the laughter of a
thousand suns joyously bursting
from your heart.

Soul Power is
cherishing you
and knowing you
are a love song to God.

Be God's Love.

It is having
a song in your heart
that is the pure creation
of God's expression.

Sing.

Soul Power is
the intoxicating nectar
of your preciousness
enheartened with life.

Celebrate Life.

It is you
fully loving you
loving another
loving the infinite
loving you.

Love Fully.

Soul Power is
being one with the
boundless flow
of interconnectivity.

Be One . . .

for in the giving, you are receiving
the greatest gift—Divine Source.

Soul Power values
the blessing
of your life
with innocence and joy.

Be Blessed.

It is knowing you yourself
must value your worth
because the only poverty is
not feeling worthy.

Know Your Worth.

Soul Power is
aware that any feeling of lack
needs to be returned
to the infinite abundance within.

Re-Turn.

*W*ithin each one of us
is a wealth beyond price,
an inexhaustible currency.

Be Wealthy.

Soul Power is

having

it all.

Enjoy the plentitude.

Have Plenty . . .

for the gift of being is priceless and
cannot be bargained nor bought.

Soul Power is
the Divine poetry
of the sensuous.

Be Divinely Poetic.

$\mathcal{J}$t is encountering God
through the ecstatic
embrace of the senses.

Be Sensitive.

Soul Power is
the burning ember
in your innermost
heart space.

Embrace Your Sacred Heart.

It is a burning desire

beyond the material realm

turning toward that Light again and again.

Be with the Eternal Flame.

Soul Power is
experiencing the more you love
the Divine
the more you know
the Divine.

Know Divinity . . .

for God's gift is your effulgent
golden heart-space, satiated with
sensorial knowing.

Soul Power is
savoring the pleasure
of paradise.

Taste the Sweetness.

$\mathcal{I}$t is letting open the gate

melting any hardness

that blocks your way.

Open the Flood Gate.

Soul Power is
repentance for any way
you locked yourself out
of your home.

Come Home.

*I*t is living to a higher octave

expanding your frequency

to limitless freedom.

Live Limitlessly Free.

Soul Power is
a sacred marriage
and a living prayer
in communion with Creator.

Live Graciously . . .

*for yours is the open-hearted rapture
and grandeur of the holy feast.*

$\mathcal{S}$oul Power is
turning toward
the One Perfection.

Turn Toward the One.

It is

returning

to the unity

of God's love.

Be in Beloved Union.

Soul Power is
being held
in the flowing embrace
of living devotion.

Be Held.

It is knowing no matter where you turn

is the face

of Beloved.

Know Love.

Soul Power is
the honeyed nectar
of spiritual abundance.

Taste the Nectar . . .

for yours is the feast of eternal
devotion and the elixir of bliss.

Gratitude is the generator of abundance in our life. Gratitude is reciprocity, which means as we give, so we receive, and as we genuinely receive, we in turn are gifting the giver. We are both gifting the giver and being gifted simultaneously. It is the reciprocal flow of Grace spontaneously inherent in our soul.

Gratitude is necessary to honor life. It leads with a glad-full heart, unifying the mind and body, allowing for the miraculous to guide us. Gratitude is important because it enlarges understanding through our heart. When we are grateful, we directly connect with Divine Source—our life becomes a living prayer. We feel satiated by the infinite supply of Divine's eternal fountain of loving Grace.

So, how do we access gratitude and free it from our limited definition of abundance?

We do this by first understanding the limited definition of abundance. This means attachment to anything external, which can be possessions, people, and places. Gratitude is free of this, and its very core is joyful. Therefore, to access gratitude, we need to feel our joy. Joy allows the playful innocence of our innate preciousness to freely flow. So, how can we have what we want and yet not grasp externally for something or shut down internally around whatever it is that we are wanting?

We do this by being both conscious of feelings around a sense of self-worth as well as being aware of the energetic direction of movement that flows through our magnetic heart center, which leads us to our sacred heart, which resides between the chest and diaphragm. We need to sense if our essential heart feels open or closed, walled off, or withheld in relation to our wants, and we need to feel both of these (the heart and wants) together at the same time. What we think and what we feel must be congruent for abundance to freely flow.

So, scarcity is the issue here. As a child, if we did not feel valued and loved unconditionally for our pure natural be-ingness (meaning if our precious nature was not mirrored back to us), then we grew up feeling that our precious being was not of value, not enough, or that there was never enough for us. In other words, we took on a scarcity consciousness. In turn, we withheld the generosity of our true essence mistakenly believing that we could protect it. Eventually we too forgot the self. We mistakenly interpreted personally another's limitations to mean that we were not loveable or that our precious nature was not as valuable as our intellect, image or prowess, and so on.

Now, from here, no matter what we say or do, it doesn't seem to work. We never seem to get what we really want because under the positive affirmations and declarations that we practice for self-improvement underlies this deep feeling of not deserving, and we will continue to unconsciously sabotage what we desire. For example, if we do make gains, we make sure that we cannot enjoy our essential self for fear of being unwanted, rejected, or feeling guilty for being happy for having what we want. To heal and grow, we have to expose our hidden self-denying beliefs.

For example, when I was an infant, my mother was ill, and I went to live with another family. This family encountered a difficult hardship of their own, and so they passed me on to other caregivers. By the time I was two years old, I had lived with five different families. As a result, in me grew a deep-seated belief that I did not belong or deserve a home. At the root of this was a feeling of not being wanted. From my young mind, I believed that it was because of me that everyone struggled. My currency for feeling self-worth was in debt. So, I grew up silently feeling that I owed others for my life. As an adult, this belief showed up with me giving away my time, my energy, my money, and not claiming financially what I had worked for and what was mine to own.

For my healing, I had to be willing to look at, and ultimately feel, my unconscious patterns that did not allow me to have what I wanted. Even though I thought I wanted something, in my body I could feel a restriction. I felt a physical sensation of a knot between my chest and my diaphragm. To access this energetic blockage, I learned to feel the sensations associated with not being wanted. When I let these sensations in and could be with the associated emotions, my physical blockage dissipated, and I could feel joy in my life and be generous without giving myself away. I had to claim my own precious-ness for the law of reciprocity to engage.

The issue here is between scarcity and generosity, and our attachment to not deserving, and these beliefs bind us in a knot. Therefore, through our work, when we discover this most inner buried place where the diaphragm and chest meet, and we feel our worthiness there, this center will open. Then, we can find here the treasure chest buried within our own chest that we had been looking for externally to fulfill us. And, here is the deal about gratitude: we must claim the inner treasure of our true self; in doing so, we receive this gift, and a well-spring releases that directly connects us with Divine Source.

It is an internal job to connect in this way, and if we do the work, we will claim and grow our appreciation for our God-given gift, our native abundance, and our joy. It does not mean that life is exempt of challenges; yet in these challenges, the feeling of our Divinity can still be experienced! Every day is a spa day when we remember to pause to appreciate and give thanks for what we have. We learn not to cut the self off from our inner abundance. We cannot afford to live in deficit, for the cost is high, and we will negate our natural resource.

Truth

Soul Power is
showing up
to the truth
no matter what.

Show Up.

It is
you being you.
It is being true
with your whole self.

Be You.

Soul Power is
whole power.
It includes
all parts of yourself.

Be Whole.

It is being

responsible

for what you create.

Be Responsible.

*S*oul Power is

the ground of your being.

It is stable

like a mountain

that supports your whole life.

Be Grounded ...

for you are a multisensory,

multifaceted clear diamond of

consciousness illuminating truth.

It is seeing reality

as it is

without distorting

the truth.

Get Real.

Soul Power is
sustainability.
It is showing up
to ways
that generate well-being.

Be Sustained.

It is letting go
of any defensiveness
that gets in the way
of your wholeness.

Let Go.

Soul Power is
asking for help
with what you
do not know how to do.

Ask for Help.

*I*t is honoring

an innate capacity

to be all you can be.

Honor Your Self…

for you are walking your talk and
committed to showing up responsibly
in every way possible.

Soul Power is

being

consistent and reliable.

Have Constancy.

It is being clear

by living awake

with healthy boundaries.

Be Clear.

Truth is sober.

Accept that fact.

You will breathe easier.

Be True.

Soul Power is
the confidence
that arises from
telling the truth.

Be Confident.

*I*t is you releasing you

from judging yourself

judging another

who is judging you

who is really judging themselves.

Release Judgement . . .

for you genuinely embody respect
for yourself and all others.

$\mathcal{S}$oul Power is
a tolerant heart.
It is having tolerance
for one another's differences.

Tolerate with Love.

*I*t is including it all.

Each one of us has

intrinsic value.

We are interconnected

all parts of a whole.

Value Wholeness.

Soul Power is surrendering
what is not congruent
and becoming truer to you.

Surrender.

It is being mindful
that your intentions
can manifest in form.

Form Pure Intentions.

Soul Power is you honoring you,

co-creating with Creator

evolving expressions of love.

Honor Yourself…

for your will is aligned with the

pure perfection and manifestation

of Divine will.

Soul Power is balance.
It is understanding
that an opposite resides
within each quality.

Be Balanced.

It is being

the container

for new possibilities.

Open to Possibilities.

Soul Power is you
birthing consciousness.
The whole universe is
yours to discover.

Be Conscious.

It is integrating
the inner and outer,
future and past,
masculine and feminine,
and heaven and earth.

Be Integral.

Soul Power lets

nothing

get in the way

of your magnificence.

Be Magnificent…

for you are diamonds upon

diamonds of infinite brilliance

and potentiality.

Soul Power is One with the Divine.

Be One.

It is

connected with

nothing and everything

at once.

Connect.

$\mathcal{S}$oul Power is
the transcendental Absolute.

$\mathcal{T}$ranscend.

It is

the still point

of

opposites.

Be still.

Soul Power is
an
everchanging
continuum.

Be the Change . . .

*for you are the transcendental
who is conscious of the Absolute
where all is manifest.*

Truth is grounded, mindful, respectful, and whole. In truth, we are committed to being accountable. If we fall, we stand. If we forget, we practice remembering. If we err, we admit to the missed step. Truth is naturally self-correcting, resilient, integral, and honorable. It is based in reality, even if no one else believes it. Truth is the foundation needed to support a fulfilling life.

So, how do we access truth? Specifically, how do we show truthfulness to the self?

We show up and be reliable. And, this starts by showing up for our self. When we practice this, we reinforce and grow self-confidence. We can count on our self to show up again and again; we have our backs. We support our self the best way we know how, and if we do not know how, we ask for help.

To be in truth is a phase in the work that requires us to consistently show up and be responsible for the choices we have made without attacking our self or another with criticism and judgmental thoughts or comments. It is the ability to see the reality of the situation as it is. In this way, we support our self to grow.

Truth is challenging to embody because at its root it is tied to our inherent wholeness. If we have not learned yet to know or trust the self, or our own good judgement, then we will wear a shield of defensiveness, like armor. This armor separates us and does not allow us to feel our truth. This can result in destructive judgement that can be very critical. This kind of judgement can appear as excessive confidence. We use our energy to hold up our armor and protect our self because we know no other way, and at some deep level, we may believe that we are not worthy or that our unknowing will be exposed. So, again, how do we begin to know truth?

First, we lay down our armor. We literally lay it down to the ground—we let go of the stance, the position, and any defensiveness to make right or wrong. Also, we need to get out of the head and trust the gut (body sensations). We have to be willing to be vulnerable. We have to be able to stand in the vulnerability of our truth. And, this can feel so exposed.

When I first began my practice, I had to learn to trust what I felt—my body sensations. Sometimes clients would be telling me one thing, but their bodies would be saying something different, and my body would be telling me to trust the message of the clients' bodies. I had to learn to trust my instincts, and to gently ask about the message that their bodies were conveying, and this was terrifying for me because I was seeing something behind their armor, and I was taking a risk in witnessing this and speaking of it.

Second, we need to understand that the judgement in truth is not critical. Instead it is like the judgement of the scales of justice in that it weighs and discerns and listens and feels the truth—through tuning into our own bodies. Our bodies speak to us. In our bodies, truth feels easeful. There is no need to armor and defend our truth, and this is how it feels in our bodies when we land in our truth. It is crisp, clear, and light. There is no confusion. It is balanced and integrated.

In contrast, a lie does not feel expansive in the body. A lie as a sensation in the body feels constricted. It comes from a place of deficiency and from the need for protection. It will feel tight. It can feel like confusion and distortion. But, the distinction between a lie and truth in the body can be challenging to discern. As in my case, growing up, I did not know how to feel truth in my body. I did not know how to trust myself. Growing up with trauma, I was confused about truth. It took me years of the practice of showing up and laying down my armor. Over time as I became more aware, and through the grace of learning from many gifted healers, I learned to feel the sensations in my body and to know how truth feels differently in my body than a lie.

Here is what I have learned—Be with the truth. Don't turn away. Be reliable. Show up—again and again. When we allow the self to be with the energetics of a feeling and let it come into focus through the body, we may perceive for instance a shield of armor ready for battle that is protecting an area in the body which feels vulnerable. That area may be a feeling of tightness. Or, maybe a wall is felt. Now we are looking at boundaries and ways we protect our body, beliefs, or feelings from trespass. Perhaps an entire fortress is built around us to defend our early and unconscious feelings of vulnerability that are buried in our body. So now we have this fortified, unconscious defense response that arises automatically any time we feel threatened.

Or, for some of us, a trespass was so violating that we split off any awareness of being embodied whatsoever and space out completely. We are in the clouds and nobody is home as the sensations and feelings of helplessness were so overwhelming. If this is your situation, please do work with a skilled somatic practitioner for support. For here our monitor of regulation is so out of balance that we need skillful professional help to get it back in balance, and we need a lot of time to develop this capacity.

Remember, in our bodies, truth is easeful and soft. If we are feeling tightness, or protection, or defensiveness, we are not in the full truth. When we feel this tightness (and all of us in this journey will), we are asked to bridge the separation and to be present with the contrasting beliefs, emotions, and energies. We are asked to be completely vulnerable and present with the truth as we feel it in our bodies.

And then, we must surrender. We surrender the self to the depth of where the truth brings us. Whatever judgement or feeling of lack it brings up, we have to be present with that. And, we cannot just think it, we have to feel it in the body too. Truth lives in the body.

We are asked to lay down our armor, again and again, in all its forms and layers. If we can show up enough to do this, over and over, and be courageous enough to lay down our armor at our feet, in the depth of the emptiness, pristine awareness arises — a fresh, clear look. In this clarity (this truth), we land and open our awareness; we come all the way down and into the self. And, in this clarity, a channel of inner consciousness connects us with the heavens and the earth through fully embodied awareness. It permeates and infuses our bones with Divine's light. And, at the same time, this inner spaciousness of awareness shines, exposing our compensatory patterns.

Here in the spaciousness of awareness we feel contained yet resilient. Breathing and being breathed all at once, we let the breath through. This awakened new quality of being contains us with the claiming of our inner light, bringing a feeling of stability, sustainability, and universal support.

And, through this process, a profound depth of awareness occurs. A new capacity that is grounded in a loving truth arises, and with it comes a wholeness that emits our diamond light brilliance. We are exposed, and in this exposure, we are uniquely brilliant.

Wisdom

Soul Power is
being the star
of your existence.

Be the Star.

It is allowing
your dazzling light
to sparkle.

Be Dazzled.

Soul Power is
sharing the magic
of your
unique expression.

Share Your Magic.

It is intrinsically

knowing

your loving presence.

Know Presence.

Soul Power is realizing

that you are more

than what has happened to you.

Be More . . .

for your radiance shimmers like
the midnight moon reflecting upon
luminous waters.

Soul Power is
you seeing you.

Be Seen.

$\mathcal{I}$t is witnessing

the light

of your existence.

$\mathcal{Y}$ou $\mathcal{E}$xist.

Soul Power is
trusting the guidance
of your inner wisdom.

Trust Your Guidance.

$\mathcal{I}$t is befriending
the mysterious unknown.

Open to the Mystery.

$\mathcal{S}$oul Power is
precisely perceiving
between
the seen and unseen.

$\mathcal{P}$erceive $\mathcal{I}$t...

$\mathit{for\ you\ are\ a\ brilliant\ vision}$
$\mathit{of\ \mathcal{D}ivinity's\ co\text{-}creation}$
$\mathit{and\ manifestation.}$

Soul Power knows
that fear is
at the root
of all defenses.

Face Your Fear.

It is letting yourself grieve
the disappointment
of where identifying with fear
has led you.

Grieve Your Loss.

Soul Power is
letting go
and not trying to control
the outcome.

Trust Falling.

It is allowing
the buoyancy
of sacred space
to catch you.

Be Held.

You have

infinite support

in ways

unexpected and unknown.

Know You Are Not Alone …

for you are a Divine instrument
traversing a multitude of dimensions.

Soul Power is
self-mastery.
It is changing
obstacles into miracles.

Believe in Miracles.

It is
discriminating wisdom.
Your words and beliefs
create your reality.

Be Discerning.

*S*oul Power knows

that only you

have the power to change

your words and thoughts.

Choose Wisely.

*I*t is the motivation

to see limitations

from a larger view.

See It All.

Soul Power is

having the patience

to wait

for the answer to be revealed.

Be Patient...

for you live from a vast, limitless,

synchronistic perfection of

interconnection.

*S*oul Power is
standing at the edge
of the precipice.
It is the paradox of identity.

Meet the Edge.

It is harnessing
your power
and not deviating
from being purely
present here.

Be Here.

Soul Power is
waking from
a nightmare of pain
and realizing the presence
of a greater you.

Wake Up.

It is being

with the great emptiness

and knowing what is essential

will be revealed.

Trust the Mystery.

It is sitting

with the deep stillness

and being calm

in the eye of a storm.

Be Still…

for your beauty resounds and

reflects a loving universe erased

of any limited identity you had

previously known.

$\mathcal{S}$oul Power is

sitting in

great and natural deep peace.

Be the Peace.

It is being
here and everywhere
at once in the timeless
eternal now.

Know All Is.

Soul Power has
access to the primordial
substance of existence.
It is the word of God.

Be the Logos.

It is knowing

that the more subtly

you touch Creation

the more your realities expand.

Expand Consciousness.

Soul Power is going deeper
beyond thought into silence
to stillness
and beyond to Source.

Welcome Source's Love …

for you are a conduit of
Creator's expression manifesting
the living intelligence of a
profoundly peaceful love.

Wisdom is the Divine Light that connects everything. It is the Universal Intelligence that unites us all. Wisdom is the mind awakened, free of projections, free of hiding behind masks of roles that we play. It is the true self, poised in faith, and is the direct guidance of self-knowing. Wisdom is visionary. It is the mystic who has evolved through self-mastery. So, when we speak of wisdom, we are really speaking to self-mastery. It is a phase in the work that requires us to drop our masks and learn to trust the essential self.

So, how do we access wisdom? Specifically, how do we show up to wisdom's positive guidance?

By patience. It takes patience because we are so deeply hidden behind our masks. These masks are the roles we play in our lives. For example, to the world, I am seen as a mother, teacher, healer, nature lover, and a host of other roles. However, these are the roles of my daily life. But, underlying all of these is an essential me that is free of any role and aligns with the Universal Light. This is my soul. So, while my roles change, there continues to be a constant sense of Self that is present at all times, no matter what role I am in.

To access wisdom, we need to access our spirit within the soul. This can be challenging because our masks are a way that we get approval. When we are validated in this way, we feel like we exist. By letting go of our masks, it is terrifying if we do not know our light, because we feel like nobody.

We feel like we do not exist. With a mask, we are asking the external world to validate us. However, from our spirit, we validate the self!

We, with patience, begin to access our wisdom by being present with our body and sensing it. For example, with practice if you listen to the words you say and pay attention to how your body responds to what you are thinking or saying, you will learn a lot about yourself. If your body is contracting with your words or thoughts, you may be identifying with a role and not your greater truth. It is through these subtle practices that we learn to access our wisdom.

Again and again, we are asked to be fully present and to not deny or manipulate our experience. We are asked to meet the edge of any discomfort related to our self-image and then back off and rest. This means we need objectivity. For example, we may identify with our work, and at times face challenges at work because others may be criticizing us. If we identify with the criticism as who we are without including objective awareness, then we can collapse from the criticism or get defensive, and we forget to access our wisdom. Whereas, if we back off and get perspective, we can connect to our wisdom and its guidance. But remember, we must be gentle and patient or we will overwhelm our system. Like labor, it takes time. It is slow and patient. There is a right timing when everything lines up—a precision, and then the beauty and magic of a new life can come through. And, when it does, we experience a tremendous sense of calm and peace, and we become truly empowered. Now we trust the self. We feel safe to be in our own skin. We no longer feel we have to fight or run or hide. Instead, we maintain our full presence.

And, this is power. We are this power. And, this power is love. With the letting go of identifying with our masks, we find that the fear of being nobody without our masks is actually a tremendous relief. We discover that we are creators in the mighty architecture of Source; we are artists, scientists, and mystics of all walks of life, and now our identity is aligned in service of the Light. Indeed, we are the star of our universe, bowing in service to the great Source of all creation.

In this place, we are held in the universal wisdom that runs through all of us. There is a palpable quality of intimacy and of connection to Creation beyond anything we experienced behind our individual masks. And, all that was required was for us to let go and let fall down the outworn structure of our images that we were still clinging on to, mistakenly calling it the self. We are not that. That is and was only a pattern. We are of the brilliance that buoys us up once we let go and fall.

With wisdom comes masterful perception, and a feeling of deep peace, evoking quality insight and clarity of mind.

Compassion

$\mathcal{S}$oul Power is

listening

with your heart.

Listen with Heart.

$\mathcal{I}$t is having the empathy

to feel

under one's skin

the heart

of one's full experience.

$\mathcal{F}eel\ \mathcal{I}t.$

Soul Power is
fully meeting
and being with
what is present.

Be Present.

It is being with what is present
without trying
to do something
to make it different.

Meet It Fully.

$\mathcal{I}$t is fully meeting
whatever it is
that is needing the touch
of gentle kindness.

Be Gentle ...

for you are as caring and kind
with yourself and others
as with a newborn.

$\mathcal{S}$oul Power is

acceptance

of the woundedness

no matter how difficult.

$\mathcal{A}ccept\ \mathcal{I}t.$

*I*t is allowing with love

the raw pain

to be seen, felt, and heard.

Love It All.

$\mathcal{S}$oul Power is

the compassion

to provide the time needed

to heal according to one's own season.

$\mathcal{A}$llow $\mathcal{T}$ime.

It is to not insist
there be growth
before there is readiness.

Be Patient.

Soul Power is
a nurturing love
that can
hold it all.

Be Held Completely . . .

*for you are providing a nurturing
environment for growing
potentialities of a new life.*

Soul Power is
noticing fault
and choosing
not to fault.

Choose Kindness.

It is

full disclosure.

It is revealing

the rawness

of the wound.

Reveal the Wound.

$\mathcal{I}$t is letting down

into the weight of sorrow.

Let Down.

Soul Power is
washing the heart
of any ignorance
and accepting forgiveness.

Be Washed.

Soul Power is letting go
of the grudge,
cracking open the earth,
and birthing a new form.

Welcome Your New Life ...

*for you have gone beyond right or
wrong into the heart of compassion.*

Soul Power is
genuine repentance and remorse
for anywhere
you created a divide.

Bridge the Divide.

It is reviewing

any feelings of regret

and atoning for what you did not

know how to do differently.

Forgive Yourself.

Soul Power is
a healing salve,
a soothing balm
softly covering and regenerating
your wounded heart.

Be Healed.

*I*t is healing through
turning and returning
to God's inexhaustible
and merciful love.

Return.

Soul Power is with full sincerity
turning to face
unconditional loving grace.

Be Forgiven . . .

for you have turned to face God
and can feel your Divine purpose.

*S*oul Power is
the blessed womb
of merciful love.

Have Mercy.

It is the

essence of

divine forgiveness.

Receive the Essence.

Soul Power is

the transformation that arises

again and again,

going through many stages.

Continuously Grow.

It is surrendering

to an organic process

that is

beyond thinking and doing.

Surrender.

$\mathcal{S}$oul Power is
humbly releasing attachment
to your self-image and physical form
and being reborn.

$\mathcal{B}e\ \mathcal{B}orn\ldots$

for you are birthed from a chrysalis
of transformation, shedding the old
and awakening the new.

Soul Power is
the emergence of
your newly discovered
potential—
a fresh start.

Emerge.

It is

being born again,

of pure body, mind, speech, and action.

Be Reborn.

Soul Power is
being sung alive
by the love song
of Divine's creation.

Be the Song.

It is the harmony
that whole healing brings
that comprises
the heart of compassion.

Be in Harmony.

Soul Power is whole love.

It is your essential love,

multi-faceted,

gracious, strong, tender, and wise.

You Are Love . . .

*for you shall eternally bloom from
the heart of Compassion's flowering.*

Compassion requires whole healing, and whole healing involves the mind, the emotions, and body sensations too. When we speak of compassion, we are really speaking to an advanced level of self growth. It is a phase in our work that requires everything of us.

So, how do we access compassion?

First of all, it is through kindness. This kindness requires that we be present with whatever the hurt or the wound is that has shown up and repeated itself throughout our life. When we feel that wound, when we feel that pang of the hurt, we really have to let that pain in. We have to let it in close to the heart. We have to meet it, and we have to be a friend to the wound—to really be willing to be present with it without judgement.

Then, we must surrender into the depth of the wound and where this brings us. So, there is going to be a sadness, an anger, or whatever is present concerning that hurt. Whatever emotion comes up, we have to be present with that. And, we cannot just think it or understand it—we have to feel it. And, when we feel the emotion and the body sensations, when we meet this, then we are asked to surrender even more. We are asked to lay it down—and to lay the self down—all the way down to the ground, to the earth of our body, of our being, and be completely present, all the way down.

In this place, just like when we snap a limb off of a branch and the sap oozes forward, our wound may ooze. It can feel awful. It may feel like the snapping off of our limb or the penetration of an attack. We have to meet the rawness that is exposed and the truth of this. We must not turn away. We are going to have to look at and be with the wound. We will need to see and feel whatever it is exposing, and it is going to be raw and open.

By staying and being present with the wound, we hit the ground. We come all the way down into the wound. It is required for us to land and penetrate the hurt. In this most inner place, we are touched in such an intimate way with a profound awareness that presents all points of view, and this is the compassion.

At the same time, as we go down and into our wound, we must also hold in a careful balance, a spaciousness to ensure that we do not get stuck in our woundedness. This inner depth of spaciousness is an objective awareness that the wound is not all and not everything, and we are more than the wound.

So, we are both with the wound and with the larger broader view. This conscious balancing allows us to see what we had not seen. We see from the eyes of the most inner self and from the eyes of the other. And, when we can be in heart with all of this, without turning away, without judging, without blaming—completely owning the full territory of this terrain—then the soft covering of this paleaku (which is Hawaiian for the soft, mossy covering of the earth) lays its healing balm on the wound, and the sap begins to cover over the wound, and from the inside out the gentle healing begins. With this gentleness of spirit, we begin to heal.

From the inside out, the full depth of healing occurs. In this process, something arises—something so full, so precious, so loving, an upwelling of love, a springing forward, and from our depth, we discover a new capacity for being.

A new capacity that is loving arises, and our heart becomes that healing balm. It is almost as though life grows, like starts of vines, from within our bones. And, it is a springing, a well spring of something so new, so alive. And from this process, from the porosity of this growth, we compost in the reality of a much larger awareness that we could not have even imagined from the mind alone. A depth and fullness of awareness occur—it's organic—it's natural—and it's inspiring.

Compassion is whole healing—mind, body, and soul.

Afterword

*May these Love Notes kindle your inspiration
and enrich connection with the blessings of
your soul's Divinity.*

Accessing the soul requires *presence*. Presence is pre-essence. Presence orients us to where we are. As we become skilled with this, a lesser known sensorial landscape emerges that awakens awareness. Here we grow the capacity to be both present and sense at the same time and in the moment; now we are *presencing*. Through presencing one eventually comes to an impasse. This is as far as the ego structure knows. It is at this place, if we can stay present, that a terrain requiring *subtler perception* unfolds revealing a more refined and delicate landscape. This is the subtle body of the soul, and its language is *essence*.

Essence, in its most simple meaning, is love. It is that place where the Divine Light in the soul meets the body. Essence supplies a precise antidote for whatever ails the mind, body, or heart. It is a specific substance, a nutritive medium, that is a gift of the soul and enables us to grow. We must consciously receive this gift that the guidance of our soul has given and in response show our appreciation. Here, essence meets essence. And, while our soul's power may appear barely perceivable, it is mightily magnificent, illuminating consciousness, where we are touched by, and in touch with, the loving nature of Divine—ushered beyond what we had previously known.

The truth is that all these qualities of presence are of the One Presence and occurring at once. It is our capacity to tap into the greater consciousness that we are developing. So, the practice here is to be aware of thoughts, emotions, and sensations. Little by little, step by step our capacity to be more present and more conscious grows:

Presence is *Open Awareness* ~ Mind

Presencing is *Embodied Awareness* ~ Mind-Body

Subtle Perception is *Attunement* ~ Mind-Body-Soul

Essence is *Soul and Spirit* ~ Divine Presence.

This book, *Soul Power*, has provided an introduction to these concepts and ultimately to our innate knowing. The accompanying *Soul Power Workbook* will expand on these concepts and will provide exercises and assistance for positively growing these areas of your life. The following are key qualities that are embedded within each chapter of *Soul Power*, and these will be further expressed in the workbook.

COURAGE ~⤳~ Expression
Red Essence
Courageous love enables tolerance to embody the charge
of passion by releasing attachment and creating
autonomous self-actualization.
Courage transmutes our emotional fire into essential strength.
Fire Nurtures Earth

GRATITUDE ~⤳~ Provision
Gold Essence
Gratitude's devotion produces self-value and joyous
abundance when we receive Divine's gift — the beloved.
Gratitude reveals the treasure within our heart's inner heart.
Earth Nurtures Metal

TRUTH ~⤳~ Container
White Essence
Truth supports integrity and reliably generates the
capacity to embody self-confidence.
Truth is the sustainer and shows the Way.
Metal Nurtures Water

WISDOM ～ Guidance
Black Essence
Wisdom's patience empowers intuitive reflection,
insightful choice, and new possibilities.
Wisdom is the alchemy of transformation.
Water Nurtures Wood

COMPASSION ～ Healer
Green Essence
Compassion's loving care and kindness heal our
wounds nurturing regeneration and new growth.
Compassion listens with heart.
Wood Nurtures Fire

Together these foundational elements of our human nature expressed through the essences of our soul comprise a cohesive map integrating thinking and feeling with intuition and sensation in unique combinations that directly affect our well-being and evolution. Knowing that our soul rests in our body, we must inhabit our body to connect with our soul. For it is here, held in the wings of the soul's love that we are lifted, and ever reminded to simply — **Be the Love** — to be who we truly are.

*Y*ou loving you,
loving the *D*ivine,
loving you!

SOUL POWER

is...strong values

is...heartful listening

is...embodied presence

is...rooted here and now

is...being mindful with love

is...letting your self be seen

is...opening to the big picture

is...truthfully walking your talk

is...expressing your inner guidance

is...trusting the path of your purpose

is...the capacity to return to wholeness

is...courageously staying in your own skin

is...surrendering to the pure intrinsic truth

is...allowing pause and waiting with patience

is...self-actualizing the inner Guidance of the soul

is...living your passion and desires wholeheartedly

is...forgiving the shortcomings of yourself and others

is...respecting boundaries about what you can or can't do

is...providing a soothing space for healing and regeneration

is...knowing that you have the support of the entire universe

is...honoring your motivations even if they do not make sense

is...choosing how to be in relationship with others in integrity

is...cherishing the gift of abundance and preciousness of each life

is...integrating any separation between your will and divine will

is...directly realizing all is love and love is the essence of all creation

is...valuing the generosity of Creator's gift and devoting your life in honor.

About the Author

I have traveled the path of self-transformation all of my life. Yet 40 years ago, I stepped into an in-depth practice of presencing and self-reflection that forever changed me. From that time on, my life became dedicated to this way of practice and being. For 17 years, I traveled internationally mentoring clients to inspire positive change and growth. A few years later I founded my school Terrain of Essence Teachings.

I have worked with thousands of clients, have taught hundreds of students who have graduated from my 3-year intensive training, and now mentor practitioners who have completed 650 hours of supervised study. My students have dubbed me midwife of the soul and a soul guide for people who have learned to directly connect with their authentic nature and core self.

The call is great in our world today to step up to our fuller potential. With the steady requests from my students, I am excited through my writing to bring this work into a form that can be shared.

Please join me and all of us on this great adventure! If you would like more information, please visit my Terrain of Essence website at terrainofessenceteachings.com.